MW00960768

WORKBOOK

For

Neurotribes

The Legacy of Autism and the Future of Neurodiversity: A Practical Guide For Implementing Steve Silberman's Book

Phenomenal Print

Disclaimer!!!

This book is a companion book designed for informational and educational purposes only. The content is based on the ideas presented in the main book but it is not endorsed or affiliated with the author or publisher of the main book.

The workbook is intended to complement and enhance the main book, offering readers additional tools for personal growth and self-reflection. However, the workbook should not be considered a substitute for professional advice, diagnosis, or treatment.

While every effort has been made to ensure the accuracy and completeness of the information in this workbook, the publisher and author assume no responsibility for errors, inaccuracies, or omissions.

Table Of Contents

How To Use This Workbook

Choose a Quiet and Comfortable Space:
Find a place that is quiet and comfortable where you can dedicate focused time to work on the workbook. Minimize distractions to enhance your concentration.

Understand the Requirements:
Carefully read the instructions and prompts provided in each section of the workbook. Ensure you have a clear understanding of the tasks and objectives before proceeding.

Use a Pen or Pencil:
As instructed, complete the workbook using a pen or pencil. This allows you to easily make notes, annotations, or corrections as needed throughout the exercises.

Take Breaks as Needed:
To prevent eye strain or physical weariness, take breaks as necessary. Step away from the workbook, stretch, and refresh your mind before returning to the tasks.

Seek Professional Guidance:
Feel free to reach out to a professional if you have any questions or concerns while working through the workbook. Seeking guidance ensures accurate understanding and application of the concepts.

Reflect on Learning:
After completing the workbook, take a moment to reflect on what you've learned. Consider how the insights and knowledge gained can be applied to your daily life, whether in personal relationships, professional settings, or broader societal perspectives.

Apply Learnings in Daily Life:
Integrate the knowledge acquired from the workbook into your daily life. Consider how the concepts discussed can shape your understanding of neurodiversity, influence your interactions, and contribute to creating a more inclusive and empathetic environment.

Consider Further Exploration:
If the workbook sparks additional interest or questions, consider further exploration of the topics covered in "NeuroTribes." The workbook serves as a starting point, and continued learning

can deepen your understanding of neurodiversity and related themes.

Celebrate Progress:
Acknowledge your efforts and the completion of the workbook. Celebrate the progress you've made in expanding your knowledge and awareness of neurodiversity.

Share Insights:
Consider sharing your insights and reflections with others who may benefit from your experiences. Engaging in discussions about neurodiversity can contribute to fostering understanding and acceptance in your community.

Overview Of The Main Book

Steve Silberman's "Neurotribes: The Legacy of Autism and the Future of Neurodiversity" is a ground-breaking examination that challenges traditional notions of autism while also providing a nuanced and complete view of neurodiversity. Silberman goes on a thrilling journey, starting with 'The Wizard of Clapham Common,' unraveling the history of autism, which was long concealed by the professionals who first identified it. From 'The Boy Who Loves Green Straws' to 'What Sister Viktorine Knew,' the story weaves through a variety of anecdotes, revealing distinct preferences, historical settings, and the development of toxic parenting, altering our knowledge of autism's complex nature.

"Fascinating Peculiarities" investigates neurodiversity, arguing that disorders such as autism, dyslexia, and ADHD are not faults, but rather natural variances in the human DNA. Silberman challenges readers to reconsider the notion of normality, promoting acceptance and understanding. 'The Invention of Toxic Parenting' examines parenting styles, and their influence on neurodivergent people, and offers practical suggestions for creating supportive settings.

In 'Princes of the Air,' Silberman highlights pioneers such as Leo Kanner and Hans Asperger, revealing their diverse perspectives that influenced autism research. 'Fighting the Monster' addresses the issues that neurodivergent people experience, encouraging empathy-building activities and advocacy techniques. 'Nature's Smudged Lines' investigates the genetic basis of neurodiversity, challenging stereotypes and inspiring personal contemplation on natural variances.

'The Rain Man Effect' examines the media's representation of autism, launching a critical examination of stereotypes and arguing for a rethinking of neurodivergent stories. 'Pandora's Box' investigates unexpected repercussions, raising ethical concerns and encouraging group discussion about neurodiversity's larger ramifications. 'In Autistic Space' promotes the development of safe and inclusive settings by providing practical solutions for developing autistic-friendly areas.

The climax, 'Building the Enterprise: Designs for a Neurodiverse World', proposes a future in which neurodiversity is valued. Readers are empowered to help create a neurodiverse society via vision board activities and action plans. Silberman promotes cooperation, networking, and personal commitments to neurodiversity, encouraging readers to actively participate in changing society's perspectives.

CHAPTER 1: THE WIZARD OF CLAPHAM COMMON

Key Lessons

Introduction to Leo Kanner: This chapter discusses Leo Kanner, a seminal figure in autism research. You learn about his work and how he helped shape early ideas of autism.

Pioneering Observations: Learn about Kanner's comprehensive observations of autistic youngsters, as well as the diagnostic criteria he developed. This lays the groundwork for future conversations about the development of diagnostic criteria.

Case Histories Narrative: Explore Kanner's tales of particular case histories, which provide insights into the unique experiences of persons diagnosed with autism throughout this time period.

Impact on Diagnostic Language: Understand how Kanner's vocabulary and characterization of autism affected diagnostic language, helping to frame autism as a rare and tightly defined disorder.

Despite Kanner's impact, the idea of autism spectrum has emerged, setting the framework for a more inclusive view of neurodiversity.

Reflection questions

How did Leo Kanner's background and attitude inform his observations and knowledge of autism?

_____

_____

_____

_____

_____

_____

_____

How did Kanner's diagnostic criteria impact early perceptions of autism, and how has this changed over time?

_____

_____

_____

_____

_____

_____

_____

Consider the case histories offered by Kanner. How did these stories help our knowledge of autism in the mid-twentieth century?

_____

_____

_____

_____

_____

_____

Examine the effect of Kanner's diagnostic language on public perception. How may the choice of certain terminology influence society's views toward people with autism?

_____

_____

_____

_____

_____

_____

Given the introduction of the autism spectrum idea, how has our knowledge of neurodiversity changed, and what obstacles remain in identifying and diagnosing autism?

_____

_____

_____

_____

_____

_____

Compare Kanner's early findings to current opinions on autism. What parallels and contrasts do you see?

_____

_____

_____

_____

_____

_____

How do you believe Kanner's efforts paved the way for future autism research and advocacy?

_____

_____

_____

_____

_____

_____

CHAPTER 2: THE BOY WHO LOVES GREEN STRIPES

Key Lessons

Introduction to Temple Grandin: This chapter discusses Temple Grandin, a prominent person in the autism community. Explore her unique viewpoint as an autistic person, as well as her contributions to our knowledge of the illness.

Sensory Sensitivities: Explore Temple Grandin's sensory experiences, notably her interest in green straws. Understand the significance of sensory sensitivities in the autism experience, as well as the value of identifying and accommodating them.

Individual Preferences: Investigate the notion of individual preferences and the importance of understanding and respecting the many ways people with autism interact with the environment. Temple Grandin's fondness for green straws offers a great illustration.

Advocacy and Education: Learn about Temple Grandin's efforts to increase autism education and awareness. Understand the significance of her work in fostering inclusion and building places that are welcoming to neurodivergent people.

Recognize the importance of accepting multiple ideas, as shown by Temple Grandin's contributions. Recognize how individual diversity, rather than being seen as a disadvantage, may benefit society.

Reflection questions

This chapter focuses on Temple Grandin's experiences with sensory sensitivity. Consider your own sensory experiences and how they influence your relationship with the surroundings.

_____

_____

_____

_____

_____

_____

Consider the idea of individual preferences, as explained in this chapter. How can society better accommodate and value the distinctive preferences of people with autism?

_____

_____

_____

_____

_____

_____

_____

Temple Grandin's preference for green straws is a distinct feature of her sensory experiences. What are your particular tastes or sensory experiences, and how do these affect your everyday life?

_____

_____

_____

_____

_____

_____

_____

Discuss how activism may help to improve autism education and understanding. How can individuals help to create more inclusive settings for neurodivergent people?

_____

_____

_____

_____

_____

_____

_____

Investigate the concept of welcoming varied ideas. How can society benefit from acknowledging and appreciating the distinct perspectives of people with autism and other neurodivergent conditions?

_____

_____

_____

_____

_____

_____

_____

Consider how Temple Grandin's work has influenced public conceptions of autism. How has her activism helped to create a more inclusive society?

_____

_____

_____

_____

_____

How can knowledge of sensory sensitivities and individual preferences be incorporated into educational and professional contexts to make them more accommodating for neurodivergent people?

CHAPTER 3: WHAT SISTER VIKTORINE KNEW

Key Lessons

Introduction to Hans Asperger: This chapter describes Hans Asperger and his contributions to our knowledge of autism. Investigate Asperger's unique viewpoint and findings on a group of youngsters he dubbed "autistic psychopaths."

Recognition of Autistic qualities: Learn about Asperger's recognition of different qualities in the children he observed, stressing their individual strengths and skills as well as obstacles.

Historical environment: Examine the historical environment in which Asperger performed his study, taking into account the sociopolitical atmosphere and its influence on autism acknowledgment and acceptance.

Ethical Considerations: Consider the ethical implications of Asperger's work, especially in light of his encounters with the Nazi state. Discuss the difficulty of distinguishing scientific contributions from historical context.

Asperger's Syndrome: Learn how Asperger's observations paved the way for the idea of Asperger's syndrome, which was eventually included in the larger autism spectrum.

Reflection questions

Consider Hans Asperger's unique viewpoint on autism. How did his observations vary from those of Leo Kanner, and what insights did he offer?

_____

_____

_____

_____

_____

Consider the characteristics that Asperger saw in the youngsters he studied. How can society better recognize and use the particular qualities of people with autism?

_____

_____

_____

_____

_____

_____

Examine the historical background in which Asperger performed his studies. How did the sociopolitical context affect the awareness and understanding of autism at the time?

_____

_____

_____

_____

_____

_____

Discuss the ethical concerns surrounding Asperger's work, particularly his dealings with the Nazi dictatorship. How do historical conditions influence our understanding of scientific contributions?

_____

_____

_____

_____

_____

_____

Asperger's syndrome, which was subsequently placed into the autism spectrum, arose from Hans Asperger's findings. How has our knowledge and categorization of autism changed since then?

_____

_____

_____

_____

_____

Consider the phrase "autistic psychopaths" used by Asperger's. How has the vocabulary and terminology around autism evolved throughout time, and what influence does this have on society's perceptions?

CHAPTER 4: FASCINATING PECULIARITIES

Key Lessons

Neurodiversity notion: This chapter presents the notion of neurodiversity, which challenges the standard medical approach of interpreting neurological variances as illnesses. Learn how disorders such as autism, dyslexia, and ADHD are reframed as normal differences in the human DNA.

Shift in Perspective: Investigate the paradigm shift in comprehending neurodiversity, recognizing that neurological distinctions are not mistakes but rather add to the richness of human diversity.

Examine the social and cultural ramifications of embracing neurodiversity, which will help to create a more inclusive and welcoming society. Consider how different ideas enrich the fabric of communities.

Recognize the neurodiversity movement's role in empowering neurodivergent persons. Discuss how self-advocacy and a positive perspective on neurodivergent experiences contribute to social transformation.

Moving Beyond Pathology: Challenge the pathology-focused approach to neurodivergent diseases, highlighting the necessity of accommodating varied cognitive styles rather than pathologizing variances.

Reflection questions

Consider the idea of neurodiversity described in this chapter. How does this viewpoint change your perception of disorders such as autism, dyslexia, and ADHD?

_____

_____

_____

_____

_____

_____

_____

Consider the paradigm shift in how neurological variations contribute to human variety. How may recognizing neurodiversity improve society's attitudes toward different cognitive experiences?

Investigate the socio-cultural consequences of neurodiversity. In what ways may appreciating varied ideas help to create more inclusive and tolerant communities?

_____

_____

Recognize how the neurodiversity movement has empowered neurodivergent people. How may self-advocacy and positive reframes of experiences help to bring about social change?

_____

_____

_____

_____

_____

_____

_____

Discuss the difficulties of a pathology-focused approach to neurodivergent disorders. How can society move away from pathologizing differences and toward tolerating varied cognitive styles?

Consider personal experiences or observations of neurodiversity in your community or workplace. How have different cognitive types helped to improve the overall dynamic?

_____

_____

Consider making practical efforts to create a
neurodiverse-friendly atmosphere that highlights
neurodivergent people's skills and unique
viewpoints. How can organizations and
educational institutions accommodate different
cognitive styles?

_____

_____

_____

_____

_____

_____

CHAPTER 5: THE INVENTION OF TOXIC PARENTING

Key Lessons

Examination of Parenting Styles: This chapter critically explores historical methods of parenting, notably those labeled as "refrigerator mothers," and their purported impact on autism development. Understand how such beliefs influence parental guilt and social judgments.

Shift in Understanding: Investigate the transition from blaming parents for their children's neurodivergence to acknowledging the impact of hereditary and neurological causes. Consider the repercussions of spreading negative preconceptions about parenting and autism.

Psychological Effects: Investigate how the "refrigerator mother" idea affects the parents of autistic children. Recognize the significance of eliminating autism misconceptions in order to help families and promote a more empathic and aware society.

Advocacy for Supportive surroundings: Recognize the significance of advocating for supportive surroundings that emphasize understanding neurodiverse perspectives above propagating harmful stereotypes. Discuss ideas for raising awareness and debunking outmoded notions.

Parental tales: Investigate personal tales of parents that defy conventional expectations and stereotypes. Recognize the bravery and perseverance of parents who advocate for their neurodiverse children.

Reflection questions

Consider the historical trend of blaming parents, especially moms, for their children's autism. How has this affected cultural ideas of parenting and neurodiversity?

_____

_____

_____

_____

_____

_____

Consider the psychological effects of the "refrigerator mother" notion on parents of autistic children. How might debunking such stereotypes help families and build a more caring society?

_____

_____

_____

_____

_____

_____

_____

Investigate your own knowledge of parenting techniques and their possible effects on neurodivergent people. How can society overcome negative prejudices and embrace a more nuanced understanding of parenting and autism?

_____

_____

_____

_____

_____

_____

_____

Recognize the value of advocating for supportive workplaces. How can people help to raise awareness and disprove outmoded notions regarding parenting and autism?

_____

_____

_____

_____

_____

_____

Consider personal stories of parents who challenged cultural standards. How can society better support and elevate the experiences of parents advocating for their neurodiverse children?

_____

_____

_____

_____

_____

_____

Discuss how our knowledge of autism has shifted from blaming parents to acknowledging genetic and neurological aspects. How might this transformation help to create a more sympathetic and informed society?

_____

_____

_____

_____

_____

Consider practical ways to create a supportive atmosphere for neurodivergent people and their families, emphasizing understanding and acceptance over perpetuating damaging stereotypes.

CHAPTER 6: PRINCES OF THE AIR

Key Lessons

Introduction to Autistic Pioneers: Learn about the lives and accomplishments of autistic pioneers like Hans Asperger and Leo Kanner. Understand their various methods of identifying and comprehending autism, which will serve as the foundation for future research and viewpoints.

Compare and contrast Asperger's and Kanner's contributions and opinions. Recognize the intricacies in their work and how it influenced the early state of autism study.

Understand the historical background in which Asperger and Kanner carried out their research. Consider the cultural and scientific forces that affected their methods and perspectives on autism.

Trace the progression of our knowledge of autism back to Asperger and Kanner's pioneering work. Recognize the intricacies and obstacles associated with identifying and diagnosing autism throughout history.

Contributions to Neurodiversity: Recognize Asperger and Kanner's pioneering work in establishing the notion of neurodiversity. Consider how their contributions shape current thinking on autism.

Reflection questions

Consider the unique techniques of autism pioneers Hans Asperger and Leo Kanner. How did these viewpoints influence early understandings of autism, and what implications do they have for current research?

_____

_____

_____

_____

_____

_____

_____

Investigate the similarities and differences between Asperger's and Kanner contributions. What aspects of their work do you think are most noteworthy, and how did they influence the course of autism research?

_____

_____

_____

_____

_____

_____

_____

Discover the historical environment in which Asperger and Kanner performed their study. How did cultural and scientific forces shape their approaches and views of autism?

_____

_____

_____

_____

_____

_____

Follow the progression of our knowledge of autism via the pioneering work of Asperger and Kanner. How have definitions and diagnosis changed over time, and what obstacles remain in characterizing autism?

_____

_____

_____

_____

_____

_____

_____

Recognize Asperger and Kanner's contributions to the idea of neurodiversity. How has their pioneering work influenced current ideas on autism and neurodivergence?

_____

_____

_____

_____

_____

Consider how historical ideas on autism affect present research and activism. How does a detailed awareness of the historical background influence current initiatives?

CHAPTER 7: FIGHTING THE MONSTER

Key Lessons

Issues Faced by Neurodivergent Individuals: This chapter delves into the many issues that neurodivergent people confront, including societal misunderstandings and difficulty navigating educational and social situations.

Empathy Development: Recognize the significance of empathy in tackling the issues faced by neurodivergent persons. Investigate activities and ideas that foster understanding and compassion.

Advocacy tactics: Learn about advocacy tactics used by people and groups to confront the social "monster" of ignorance and bigotry. Recognize the potential of collective action in producing good change.

Explore the importance of supporting networks in empowering neurodivergent people. Recognize the importance of building communities that recognize and advocate for the rights and needs of neurodivergent people.

Recognize the significance of building inclusive settings that suit varied needs. Discuss how to make educational and employment environments more accessible and inclusive.

Reflection questions

Consider the issues raised in this chapter that neurodivergent people encounter. How can society better grasp and respond to these challenges?

_____

_____

_____

_____

_____

_____

_____

Explore the chapter's empathy-building activities and viewpoints. How can individuals actively create empathy to help neurodivergent people in their communities?

_____

_____

_____

_____

_____

Explore advocacy tactics used to challenge social ignorance and prejudice. How can our collaborative efforts help to bring about good change and build a more inclusive society?

How can communities and organizations create supportive settings that advocate the rights and needs of neurodiverse people?

_____

_____

_____

_____

_____

_____

What particular measures may be used in educational and business contexts to make them more accessible and inviting to neurodiverse people?

_____

_____

_____

_____

_____

_____

Consider your own experiences or observations of social issues encountered by neurodivergent people. How can people help to raise awareness and break down obstacles in their communities?

CHAPTER 8: NATURE'S SMUDGED LINES

Key Lessons

Genetic Variations in the Human Genome: Investigate the idea that neurodivergent diseases, such as autism, are caused by natural variations in the human genome rather than mistakes. Understand how genetics shapes neurological differences.

Rethinking "Errors of Nature": Challenge the notion that neurodivergent diseases are mistakes or abnormalities by framing them as part of the rich tapestry of human experience. Consider how this viewpoint affects cultural views and inclusion.

Biological foundation of Neurodiversity: Investigate the biological foundation of neurodiversity, specifically how genetic variants contribute to individuals' distinct cognitive profiles. Recognize the importance of understanding and appreciating these differences.

Implications for Diagnosis and Treatment: Consider the consequences of treating neurodivergent diseases as natural variations. Discuss how this viewpoint could alter diagnostic criteria, therapeutic options, and social support for people with different cognitive experiences.

Recognize the paradigm shift from pathologizing differences to recognizing them as inherent components of human variety. Investigate how this adjustment may reduce stigma and increase acceptance.

Reflection questions

Consider the idea of neurodivergent disorders as inherent differences in the human genome. How does this approach challenge conventional wisdom, and what consequences does it have for comprehending differences?

_____

_____

_____

_____

_____

_____

_____

Challenge the idea that neurodivergent disorders are faults or abnormalities. How does seeing these illnesses as part of the varied human experience affect society's attitudes and inclusivity?

_____

_____

_____

_____

_____

_____

_____

_____

Explore the biological underpinnings of neurodiversity. How do genetic variations influence people's distinct cognitive profiles, and how can society better identify and appreciate these differences?

_____

_____

_____

_____

_____

_____

_____

Consider how perceiving neurodivergent diseases as natural variances affects diagnosis and therapy. How may this viewpoint affect diagnostic criteria, treatment procedures, and support systems?

_____

_____

_____

_____

_____

_____

Consider the paradigm shift from pathologizing variations to seeing them as part of the natural range of human variability. How may this move help to reduce stigma and promote more acceptance in society?

_____

_____

_____

_____

_____

_____

_____

Investigate personal experiences or observations of how accepting neurodiversity as a natural difference may benefit people and communities. How might this knowledge help to create a more inclusive and empathic society?

_____

_____

_____

_____

_____

Discuss the importance of education and awareness in spreading the concept that neurodivergent diseases are natural variances. How can people and groups actively work to shift views and promote a more inclusive society?

CHAPTER 9: THE RAINMAN EFFECT

Key Lessons

Media Representation and Stereotypes: Examine how media representation influences social attitudes toward autism, especially through the perspective of popular culture. Recognize the role of stereotypes and the "Rain Man" effect in affecting public perception.

Investigate the unintended repercussions of media depiction, such as the reinforcing of limited preconceptions and the overshadowing of varied and real experiences of people with autism.

Advocacy Against Stereotypes: Recognize the significance of advocacy activities to challenge and reshape stereotyped depictions of autism in the media. Recognize the importance of media literacy in promoting more accurate and inclusive representations.

Diversity of Autistic Experiences: Emphasize the wide diversity of experiences within the autistic community, debunking the myth that a single story can reflect the complexities of autism. Accept a more complex and customized understanding.

Impact on Stigma: Discuss how media depiction impacts the stigma associated with autism, as well as how neurodiverse people are regarded and treated in different social circumstances.

Reflection questions

Consider how media depiction influences your views of autism. How have media depictions changed your knowledge, and how do they contribute to stereotypes?

_____

_____

_____

_____

_____

_____

How can limiting preconceptions overshadow the different experiences of people with autism, and why is it important to oppose these representations?

_____

_____

_____

_____

_____

_____

_____

Consider how advocating against stereotypes may help to reshape media depictions of autism. How can people and organizations help to create more accurate and inclusive portrayals?

_____

_____

_____

_____

_____

_____

_____

Consider the variety of autistic experiences discussed in the chapter. How might gaining a more nuanced grasp of individual experiences help to break down stereotypes?

_____

_____

_____

_____

_____

_____

_____

How does media affect society's views toward neurodiverse people, and how may this effect be mitigated?

_____

_____

_____

_____

_____

_____

_____

How can people actively interact with media
material to encourage accurate and respectful
representations?

_____

_____

_____

_____

_____

_____

How may education and awareness programs help people distinguish between accurate depictions and stereotypes?

_____

_____

_____

_____

_____

_____

_____

_____

CHAPTER 10: PANDORA'S BOX

Key Lessons

Unintended repercussions of Advocacy: Investigate the unintended repercussions of advocacy activities, especially in light of the rise in autism diagnoses. Recognize the intricate relationship between advocacy, awareness, and the medicalization of neurodivergent experiences.

Ethical Considerations in Diagnosis: Examine the ethical issues underlying the diagnosis of neurodivergent diseases. Examine the balance of offering assistance and resources while avoiding overdiagnosis or pathologizing normal deviations.

Diverse viewpoints on Diagnosis: Emphasize the variety of viewpoints among the autistic community on the advantages and disadvantages of diagnosis. Recognize that individuals' experiences and viewpoints differ, underlining the significance of tailored approaches.

Medicalization of Neurodiversity: Discuss the possible hazards and advantages of medicalizing neurodivergent diseases. Consider the effects on people, families, and society as a whole.

Societal Responses: Investigate societal reactions to the growing understanding and diagnosis of neurodivergent disorders. Discuss how communities may promote awareness, inclusion, and support for those with different cognitive experiences.

Reflection questions

How has improved understanding influenced the diagnosis of neurodivergent diseases, and what ethical concerns arise?

How can society achieve a balance between offering assistance and resources while avoiding overdiagnosis or pathologizing natural variations?

How do individual experiences and perspectives differ, and what does this variation tell about the complexities of neurodiverse experiences?

Discuss the possible hazards and advantages of medicalizing neurodivergent diseases. How does medicalization affect individuals, families, and society's perspectives of neurodiversity?

_____

_____

_____

_____

_____

How can communities promote awareness, inclusion, and support for those with different cognitive experiences?

_____

_____

_____

_____

_____

_____

Consider how education and knowledge influence society's views about neurodivergent disorders. How might educated and empathic approaches help to reduce stigma and promote acceptance?

_____

_____

_____

_____

_____

_____

CHAPTER 11: AUTISTIC SPACE

Key Lessons

Explore the significance of building safe and inclusive settings for neurodivergent people. Recognize how environmental elements influence the well-being and comfort of people with autism.

Developing autistic-friendly spaces: Learn about ways to develop spaces that meet the sensory demands and preferences of people with autism. Consider how careful design may improve access and quality of life.

Community engagement: Discuss how community engagement may help to improve knowledge and acceptance of neurodiversity. Recognize the importance of teamwork in developing settings that can support a variety of cognitive experiences.

Advocacy for Autistic-Friendly Environments: Learn about advocacy activities aimed at encouraging the construction of autistic-friendly environments. Consider how such projects may break down barriers and challenge societal conventions.

Highlight the relevance of encouraging autistic self-advocacy in space design and execution. Recognize the skills and ideas that neurodiverse people offer to the discussion about developing inclusive settings.

Reflection questions

Consider the necessity of building safe and inclusive environments for neurodivergent people. How might smart environmental design improve the well-being and comfort of people with autism?

_____

_____

_____

_____

_____

_____

Explore ideas for creating autistic-friendly surroundings. How can smart design increase accessibility and the general quality of life for people with autism?

_____

_____

_____

_____

_____

Consider the importance of community engagement in promoting knowledge and acceptance of neurodivergent people. How might cooperation help to create settings that accept various cognitive experiences?

Consider advocacy activities focused on creating autistic-friendly places. How might such projects help break down barriers and challenge cultural norms?

_____

_____

_____

_____

_____

_____

_____

Recognize the significance of encouraging autistic self-advocacy in the design and execution of environments. How might neurodivergent people's knowledge and insights help to create more inclusive environments?

_____

Investigate personal experiences or observations of situations that are supportive to neurodivergent people. How might people and communities actively participate in the establishment of such spaces?

Discuss the possible obstacles to adopting autistic-friendly designs in different environments. How can society address these issues and seek to make public areas more inclusive for neurodiverse people?

CHAPTER 12: BUILDING THE ENTERPRISE: DESIGNS FOR A NEURODIVERSE WORLD

Key Lessons

Explore the vision for a neurodiverse society that values and respects the distinct abilities and viewpoints of neurodivergent people. Consider the possible social advantages.

Empowerment via Design: Learn how design principles may help neurodivergent people by building places that promote variety and accommodate different cognitive types. Recognize the beneficial effects on mental health and general well-being.

Perform a vision board activity to create and explain personal and community aspirations for a neurodiverse society. Investigate the potential of imagining a world that values inclusiveness and acceptance.

Action Plans for Implementation: Create action plans to deploy neurodiverse-friendly designs in a variety of settings, including education, the workplace, and public spaces. Consider realistic actions to promote a more inclusive society.

Cooperation and Networking: Highlight the significance of cooperation and networking in achieving the goal of a neurodiverse world. Recognize the importance of collaborative efforts and partnerships in bringing about long-term, meaningful change.

Reflection questions

Consider the vision for a neurodiverse future offered in this chapter. How can a culture that values and accommodates neurodiversity help both people and communities?

_____

_____

_____

_____

_____

_____

Investigate how design principles might help neurodivergent persons. How can careful design improve mental health and well-being?

_____

_____

_____

_____

_____

_____

_____

Use the vision board activity to picture personal
and group objectives for a neurodiverse society.
What parts of inclusion and acceptance are most
important to you, and how can you help achieve
these goals?

_____

_____

_____

_____

_____

Create action plans to adopt neurodiverse-friendly designs in all sectors of life. How can real changes be made in schools, the workplace, and public areas to promote a more inclusive society?

Consider how cooperation and networking may help realize the goal of a neurodiverse society. How might collaboration and partnerships help to bring about long-term and meaningful change?

_____

_____

_____

_____

_____

_____

_____

Reflect on personal experiences or observations of situations that support the goal of a neurodiverse world. How can people actively support the achievement of this goal in their communities?

_____

_____

_____

_____

_____

_____

_____

Discuss the possible problems of adopting neurodiverse-friendly designs and action plans. How can society address these issues and seek to create a more inclusive and welcoming environment for neurodivergent people?

_____

_____

_____

_____

_____

_____

_____

Final Evaluation Questions:

How has reading "NeuroTribes" helped you comprehend autism and neurodiversity?

_____

_____

_____

_____

_____

_____

In what ways has the book challenged or broadened your understanding of the historical narratives surrounding autism research?

_____

_____

_____

_____

_____

_____

_____

How has your understanding of the variety of autistic experiences changed as you've read through the chapters?

_____

_____

_____

_____

_____

_____

How do you think pioneers such as Leo Kanner and Hans Asperger influenced society's views regarding autism?

_____

_____

_____

_____

_____

_____

How have the book's chapters on media representation changed your opinions on how autism is portrayed in popular culture?

_____

_____

_____

_____

_____

_____

_____

How do you view the influence of social misunderstandings, particularly those about parenting, on the experiences of neurodivergent people?

_____

_____

_____

_____

_____

_____

How might the notions of neurodiversity and inherent differences in the human genome help to promote inclusion and acceptance?

_____

_____

_____

_____

_____

_____

_____

Consider the unforeseen repercussions of advocacy addressed in the book. How may improved awareness affect the diagnosis and assistance of neurodiverse people?

_____

_____

_____

_____

_____

_____

_____

How might the construction of safe and inclusive spaces, as explored in subsequent chapters, benefit the well-being of neurodivergent people in a variety of settings?

_____

_____

_____

_____

_____

_____

_____

Consider how community engagement might help build understanding and acceptance. How may collaborative efforts help to break down obstacles for neurodivergent people?

_____

_____

_____

_____

_____

_____

_____

How has the book changed your perspective on the medicalization of neurodivergent conditions? What dangers and rewards do you see in this process?

_____

_____

_____

_____

_____

_____

_____

In the closing chapters, while discussing the vision
for a neurodiverse future, what components of it
connect with your own beliefs and ambitions for a
more inclusive society?

_____

_____

_____

_____

_____

_____

Consider the impact of empathy-building activities and viewpoints, particularly in Chapter 5. How might empathy help to better serve neurodivergent people?

_____

_____

_____

_____

_____

_____

_____

How could the material in the book affect your relationships with and understanding of neurodiverse people in your personal or professional life?

_____

_____

_____

_____

_____

_____

_____

Given the book's different perspectives and experiences, what measures can you take to help make society more inclusive and welcoming of neurodivergent people?

_____

_____

_____

_____

_____

_____